Samsara Town

Sean Lause

ISBN: 978-81-19228-42-3

First Edition: 2023
Rs. 200/-

Cyberwit.net
HIG 45 Kaushambi Kunj, Kalindipuram
Allahabad - 211011 (U.P.) India
http://www.cyberwit.net
Tel: +(91) 9415091004
E-mail: info@cyberwit.net

Printed at Vcore.

For my son, Christopher, with love

I would like to thank Tom Beery and Will Wells for all their wise advice as I wrote these poems.

“The universe pours moments of joy all around…among sorrow, O among sorrows.” *—Jack Kerouac*

“I’ve spoken of unworkable formulas and possibly the most unworkable formula is the whole concept of a dualistic universe.”

–William S. Burroughs

‘Anywhere is everywhere.”

—William Carlos Williams

Some of the poems in *Samsara Town* have appeared in literary journals, among them:

"Done gone blind"—*Poem, Kaleidoscope*

"A brief history of man"—*Commonsense 2*

"Why I read *Famous Monsters of Filmland" Down in the Dirt Magazine*

"Cold dark lake"—*Haiku Harvest*

"Cat in freezing rain"—*Shamrock*

"December rain" *Shadow Poetry*

"Leftover leaves"—*Poem*

"Bird lights"—*Commonsense 2* *FutureCycle Press*

Preface

Welcome to Samsara Town:

Samsara Town, a place of suffering and beauty, does not exist on any map. Its people are lonely and to this day peer through their window curtains to steal moments from each other's lives.

This perception splits us, the citizens of Samsara town, in two—observer and observed, inside and outside, illusion and reality, and this confirms our loneliness.

Our downtown square is peopled with ghosts and nowhere fire escapes, chessboards used by the homeless for shelter in the rain, movie theaters made of darkness, bats, and empty seats. Our once-thriving factories were shipped overseas, it seems centuries ago—and yesterday, for time lacks a language for loss. The rings of steel around our town that once brought jobs and tourists now seem merely a prison.

And yet, the citizens of Samsara town love and endure, though an old poet who wanders our streets insists it is all a dream. Others believe that if only the right language could be found, the town might grow green again.

Contents

Samsara Town

1960—
greengoldredbluewhitelights
strung round the towers of Sinclair Oil
like psychotic Christmases,
sawhead factories welded in steel.
smokestack missiles steaming for launch,
slouched-hat powerhouses bogarting butt-ends
diesel trains crouching, waiting for release,
endless time whistles maddening the air,
Westinghouse windows sprouting with machines,
the gas oven whispering to the H-Bomb,
a vast mechanical womb of war.
All of this is empty.

60 years later—
the Christmas lights have unstrung gone.
By night the factories
are abandoned battleships.
By dawn, a graveyard
of rust and broken cars,
the workers all turned to ghosts
bumming for rides on invisible trains
down the scars of the ripped-up tracks,
a spider-less web, a gasp and cry
of silence.
All of this is holy.

What if the Red King awakens?

seven and a half years old exactly,
I nightmare myself to a scream,
watching Alice's Red King stir, stretch,
and swallow my whole world with a yawn.
And I? In that terrible dream,
whether the King's dream, or mine,
I fold up like a telescope,
and fade with a wave into nowhere,
like the White Knight's final song.
Here is a mirror I may enter—or not,
escape into a timeless make-believe.
Yet the grandfather clock appears unsure,
Since mirrors turn everything backwards,
verdict first, trial second,
then off with all our heads!
And this mirror floats in a chessboard's light and shade,
descends endlessly, like the cry of a passing train,
as my grandmother rocks in a corner of the ceiling,
floats from her chair deep in the past,
turns into my mother, dreaming in a book,
and I am that book, fated with words.
And there's the Mad Hatter, blaming HIM,
and here am I in my alone, grandfather dead,
his raven and his writing desk abandoned,
And I am as confused as the White Queen.
wondering which is world, which is mirror,
and those books there are written backwards too:
"Amen to Artillery" becomes "Artillery to Amen."
An encyclopedia for the mad.

That stairway leads somewhere outside the frame,
to a rabbit hole fall or a hidden room,
or to a trial I will never understand.
I may not find my way inside or out,
though I'm certain I don't belong
here, there, or anywhere.
This world seems all stuff and nonsense.
The grandfather clock tells all the wrong time,
It is both there and absent, like a memory.
Yet I suspect it knows something it is not telling,
has something it longs to announce…
It tries, whirrs, begins to try to speak,
like an old man clearing his throat,
but then it falters, returns to unrevealing,
pressing one silent finger to a shhhhhhh…

Hotel Breakers

The sea, the sea is breaking apart—
Oh mother, where are all the sails?
Shh, darling, shh…
tides come in, tides return,
our sleep is their song.
I cannot sleep…
the moon, sweet mother,
Grandfather's dying face…
Sleep, my love, just sleep,
Listen to the silence
dreaming.
Mother, a moonlit skeleton
is dancing on the waves!
It cannot hurt us
here, my child,
it dances all alone.
She soothes my cheek
with her gentle hand
and whispers in my ear:
The sands go shh, shh, shhh…
The stars weave us, love,
into their web of dreams…
And the sea is both our voices now,
my son, it sets us free.

My mother's universe

My mother glues the night sky to my ceiling,
a phosphorescent universe of love,
radiating my heart to purity,
red Mercury, pearl Venus, gold Jupiter,
silver Saturn, green Neptune
with his sea of stars, Uranus and
poor old distant Pluto purple cool.
Some enchanter has woven her art here,
and now my whole room glows,
as the ceiling comes to life,
pulsing with the blood of other worlds.
How I long to climb them one by one!
I grace to the breathing of their gentle light,
and I can hear my heart beat as they fade.

Summer of War

It's a death cult—1962,
more afraid of love than of war,
and every effort they make to protect us
from the wars they dream in their soup
backfires, the more security, the more fear,
the more fear, the more security,
and so on to infinity.
Miss Van Braun, our first-grade teacher,
creeps like a crab to the window, peers, gasps,
points—"Here come the Russian bombers!"
She is really quite imaginative, and we duck
and cover beneath our wooden desks, mine
lined with lead pencils I've filched from all over
the school, my own private bomb shelter, to Hell
with everyone else it was all about saving yourself,
once I asked Miss Von Braun what I should do
if the Russians attacked while I was in the hallway
and she said stick your head inside your locker.
I did. It stayed there for eighteen years,
and never learned a thing.
At home my bomb shelter's beneath my bed,
where I creepshiver with the dusty spiders,
Campbell's Soups I swiped from my mother's cupboard,
a slingshot, a Bible, my bag of marbles, a Superman comic book,
a transistor radio where Brian Wilson also hides in his room,
in his room from the Mean Old Man,
and a box of Greenie Stickem Caps,
which I use to explode the spiders
when they start to explore me, biting.

There is an endless supply of spiders,
and an endless supply of Stickem Caps.
I should be given a medal
for my contribution to the munitions industry.

My friends and I are a walking arsenal.
The things we carry:
—A year's supply of Greenie Stickem Caps.
—20 M-80 firecrackers, for larger insects
and smaller animals oh the karma demerits I've earned.
—Three Brown Bess Daniel Boone long rifles
—Three "Ole' Betsy" Davy Crocket long rifles
—Twelve Matt Dillon six-shooter cap guns
--One General Custer six-shooter cap gun we're all afraid to touch.
—One Winchester '92, first used by Chuck Connors in "The Rifleman"
to murder half the population of North Fork, Arizona.
—Ten World War One .45 automatics that fire soft plastic pellets.
—Ten World War Two burp guns
—Ten M-I rifles with multiple-cap clips.
—A .30 caliber machine gun that fires hard plastic pellets
—A nuclear missile we made ourselves from discarded
Crest toothpaste tubes and firecrackers
though the first and only test fire trial did not
go well the missile shot straight up and came straight
down on our heads, showering us with purple sparks
and setting our hair on fire.

Our mortal enemies, the boys from the next block over, carry all of these, plus a set of Mattel walkie-talkies which they use to pinpoint infiltrations and ambushes. They are depraved monsters who deserve death.

Both sides carry:
—G.I. Joe dolls

— Ken dolls (for bayonet practice),
—Ten packs of plastic Civil War soldiers (60 Union, 40 Confederate)
—Ten packs of plastic Battle of the Little Big Horn soldiers (70 for Custer, 30 for Crazy Horse),
—Ten packs of plastic World War Two soldiers (60 American, 40 Japanese)
—One Lionel electric train armed with plastic ICBM missiles.
--One Whamo Nuclear Mop-Up Kit.

We are an armed madhouse, see, so we win World War Three
by kidnapping one of the walkie-talkie kids, tying him
to a chair and forcing him to guide his boys to a rendezvous with death—
My idea, my strategy, my victory, which is good, since I am not aware in 1962 they are getting us all ready for Vietnam. In 1965, though, I bought one pack of plastic Vietnam War soldiers (100 American, 0 Vietcong).
The enemy had become invisible. This kept me up nights. And my bomb shelters were of no help at all.
By 1971 we were coming home in boxes (Five soldiers, five boxes per neighborhood army). Why didn't they tell us that plastic bullets won't work? So we lost that war in reality, but in our imagination, oh, our imagination! We had been trained to kill so pure.

A brief history of capitalism

1961
my brother and I
set up a lemonade stand,
seven cents a glass.
On the second day,
my brother raises the price one cent.
On the third day, I design a plan:
Dilute the pitcher, make twice the profit.
On the final day, Mike Larue rides up on his bike
with his orange hair, pimples, and gnarled teeth,
pokes a sharpened popsicle stick under my chin,
and rides away with all our pennies.
Of the three of us, only Mike Larue
was a business genius.
Where is he today?
Perhaps in prison.
Perhaps on the board of directors
of a Wall Street firm.

The escape artist

Eight years old I'm Harry Houdini,
evading locks and prisons in my mind.
Escape is necessary, since fear corners me
like a giant spider, or irradiated scorpions
crawling through my veins.
I lie in the basement handcuffed and trussed
by my brother, at my request and dare,
beneath our parents' stomps and screams,
years before his death from cancer. He leaves
to play baseball, and forgets I'm here.
I'm not safe here in my parents' house.
I have to be free to at least escape
to the bomb shelter in the library basement
with its Gideon's Bible, dried eggs, and fire extinguisher.
So I kick and writhe and cry—no good.
Any second the bomb fallout may come,
glowing like sand in God's cruel hourglass,
an apocalypse critical-massing from the Empire Ape Building
to San Francisco Earthquake suicide Golden Gate Bridge,
caught in a giant octopus-embrace.
My eyes fill with twin mushroom clouds
that climb my alien-teeming brain,
and Godzilla's out there munching on trains,
banging his big tail on refugees, clicking his claws,
and glowing beyond extinction.
But I can——disappear!
My only magic trick that ever worked,
because Miss Todd, our third grade teacher,
liked to hang signs on us: "I talk too much,'

"I'm slow," "I'm lazy," "I don't play well with others."
The last sign was me, another pendent sinner.
So one day I wrote my own sign: "I am invisible,"
and disappeared for good, shut up like a telescope,
lost in the mind of the wind, as it bends the leaves
green to white, predicting distant storms.

And now I'm hidden everywhere,
in the yearning seas, and the countless air,
freeing myself from that ancient fear,
and singing to you, unlock your mind—
An artist should be a magician in love.

Samsara in Woolworth's

A Slinky on an escalator
comprehends eternity,
perpetual motion, yet metal feels no pain.
And I must travel from floor to floor
of this dime store they call reality.
Look there. There's blood all over the war toys.
Dachau mannequins,
lifeless and bald,
stare blankly at the prisoned birds.
In the spymirrors,
background is foreground,
samara is nirvana.
And yet, kids ignore the plastic monsters.
There's so much horror outside.
H-bombs praying for the Satan cloud.
Here are Band-Aids for the Holocaust,
aspirin for our mental breakdowns,
and a string of rainbow suckers out of reach.
Possible all your darkest imaginings.
They're all true, all your darkest dreams,
a place for bargains and conveyor groans.
The escalator winds round and round,
brings us ever back to beginnings,
fears our way to scarlet exits.
Why must a wound ever heal?
It is a wound's dharma to bleed.
Like escalator steps descend to nowhere,
and the world says "round and round,"
and the wars keep coming, and the empty
counter chairs say, "We're hungry and alone."

Fish cleaning

I had hoped the pull
on my slender line
was some shy sea maiden
tempting me back to innocence.
But my father's rule was clear
You catch it, you clean it, you eat it,
or go hungry.
Now his knives, bone-handled,
lie glittering like snake eyes in the sun,
and my fish lies on the wood cutting board,
motionless as leaves in moonlight.
Its eyes seem to watch me as my father's huge hand
guides mine down the silver seam,
and I feel the universe split open,
and spill its secrets in my hands.
Its organs ooze in rich profusion, slimy jewels,
the heart the round of a ring, my stomach clenches.
My father's hand is strong and sure.
I hear his breathing, round me and above.
Later, I sit alone under a maple bleeding autumn.
I look away from my fish, at the crocodile green lake.
A distant curtain of rain slips down the horizon like a thief.
Now back, I must look back, I must see my creation.
I look and look at my fish, all hunger,
and through tears watch my fingers
pluck the white feathers of its flesh,
like Adam, one day out from paradise.

Why I loved *Famous Monsters of Filmland*

The cockroaches came down as if on strings,
my father said, like some evil entertainment,
as I hid inside my monster magazine.
They dropped on your head, wriggled down your back,
or fell—hello there—into your breakfast,
when you had food in that damned tenement.
Chicago, 1934, he said.
At night the rats came waltzing in the walls,
pound those walls they scatter, never leave.
Later you hear them gnawing at the wires.
His Old Man surrendered. Beat it. Scrammed.
Sometimes sent postcards from towns so small
even the graveyards cried to get out.
My father stayed put. Never surrendered,
built our house brick by brick, board by board.
Nailed. Sawed. We did. The walls went up strong.
His dream. Not a rat or roach in sight.
Still I hid inside my monster book. Why?
Because if one wall sighed, my father twitched
a neck muscle, his head a ball turret.
Once, I left a pizza box in the sink.
He howled and gassed the whole house with home-
made poison that killed everything that crawled.
I watched his hands quiver like frightened animals.
Sometimes I heard him screaming in his sleep.
Sometimes I dreamed of cockroaches,
approaching on tip-toe, rats shhhhhing
through the walls of fears and whispers.
So when I could not sleep, I'd sneak a

flashlight under the covers and read my
Famous Monsters of Filmland, whose horrors
were contained in frames, shown to be unreal,
and whose monsters I could merely toss away.

Let dreams begin

My mother, eighteen, dreaming on her bike,
(Not yet dreaming me), down a country road,
skirt billowing, hair flowing free,
sways to the music of the sun.
Looking ahead, she stands and pedals until her thighs
quiver like bird wings testing flight. Then she—
coasts—watching the treetops float by.
She spots my father walking up the road,
trailing his long shadow in the dust.
He is thirst. He is hunger.
He is darkness longing for the light.
He sees her now—his breath unfolds,
and his whole world opens to let her in,
his bright angel of bicycles.
And yet—once she enters his wounded heart
she may never, ever return.
All his words are exiles, this abandoned son,
scarred by poverty, beaten by nuns,
his longing insatiable, oh lost, oh winds,
and I will bear the burden of their pain.
Yet she is in his arms now and all's alive.
No return, and I must one day come.
So let her brave that darkness, she is strong.
Let his kiss come thrilling through her blood.
Let her come breathless free, all reckless.
Let love dare entrance into time.
Spin this moment to threaded gold,
and may they learn a suddenness of grace.

Ohio Caverns satori

Teeth of a giant will not do,
nor great jaws of mawing,
unfathomed depths.
This is not for tourists, I think.
No words I've ever known
can embody this fear.
The dark depths fall away
somewhere between memory
and madness,
an emptiness
bleeding light,
as if all the earth were pain.
I stand here with my parents and brother,
the guide speaking geology to echoes,
and all I know
is one wrong step
and I will tumble through inner space,
following my scream to Hell.
The guard turns off the switch to let us know,
and I'm falling with no above or below
yet unafraid, with sudden calm and held,
free as forever, in a sudden love,
for I am falling through heaven,
endless silence and light.

Lessons in color composition

The palette: 1970, Samsara Senior High
student council requests a free day
to honor Martin Luther King—no dice—
The Superintendent claims Martin sub-ranks
Christopher C., that man with a dream backed by guns,
who chopped off fingers of Arawak children
who failed to find him gold…
We protest, stage walkout, the governor
sends in tanks—*tanks*—to patrol "that" end
of Samsara, where "those people" live.
Samsara Town, incorporated,
This ain't no hallelujah town.
Brushstrokes soaked in pain
that overflows the canvas.
No objective correlative could ever contain
the fear and rage and doubt and hunger,
smashed glass and toppling trophies
as our school protest goes to smash
as "The White Shirts"—mostly those
about to flunk out—start throwing mace
and swinging Louisville Sluggers.
Now a broad stroke of blood brushes the halls,
while most of us try to escape but now
cops the size of blind assumptions
invade through every door.
Batons and switchblades bite the air,
staining the canvas black and red and blue,
the colors run, the painter's clearly mad.
Miss Megaton, the physics teacher

screams this is no way to conduct a holocaust
but she can't remember where the old bomb shelter
is, or was, or maybe it's really downtown
under the Masonic temple?

Throw away the brushes, grab the tube of paint,
and stab the canvas with explosions.
Now you're completely outside the frame,
painting your fear in the air.
The entire English Department heads for the basement,
trailing footnotes and dead forms. I watch three
white swans escape through the air vent with W.B. Yeats,
Lord Tennisanyone, and George Lincoln Rockwell.
The Catholic League of Decency stands silent sentinel,
favoring mass incarceration over mass incarnation.
Salvation for all is far too democratic.
Crawling like butterflies in chains,
some of us make it outside, barely alive.
I being white am lifted by painted angels
and placed in the Walt Whitman grass
sketched in like an afterthought,
since art should at least hint of Spring.
The sun is a black widow spider,
with a tear of blood on its back.
Black is not a shade, it is alive.
White is a color without a soul,
and cannot make up its mind.
Red is not a color, is blood.
What color is madness?
Smash the painting and you'll be free.

Taking the shortcut home

The clink, er, clinic psychiatrist,
the-rapist, uh, therapist,
shepherd of minds and souls,
blesses me with a tender, have-a-seat palm
and informs me I sometimes have difficulty
distinguishing illusion from reality,
"the demon from the dream."
I would agree with him,
but I'm not certain he's really here.
The mindfulness coach does her Buddha best
to keep me from losing my mind.
But I keep forgetting the Four Noble Truths—
All but the first—All Life is Suffering."
That one never leaves me—plays for days,
because I see it working everywhere—
as arrogant as a blind assumption—
from the worm crawled from flood to sidewalk
to my grandmother's last wild stare.
I tried to put an end to Maya and me.
Illusion or no, I tossed myself from our house,
age 17, aiming for the stark white rocks below.
Missed. God. Damn. It. Missed.
Landed on a startled sunflower instead.
I have half a hunch that sunflower was real,
but confess I had never really looked at a sunflower.
I lay breathing the clouds in and out, covered in seeds
and mysteries, singing for the sun to take me home.

Learning to swim in Lake Erie

Everyone is having fun but me.
I can't understand it.
Perhaps this sun is too bright for thought,
or the amusement park rides all round us
are flooding the air with screams and laughter
so all my thoughts are drowned.
My young wife is teaching me to swim.
She dives and resurfaces like a seal,
a spindrift of pure joy, her sky mousseline.
I kick and thrash and gasp and flail behind,
the horizoned blue an army of shields,
all those glitterwaves careless of death.
Seagulls call and cry their exile,
cast like heretics to the mindless winds.
This great lake I am trying so hard to enter
is ringed in rollercoasters, torn tickets,
cotton candy hearts and desperate laughter.
She is calling to me in words I cannot hear.
My life has been mostly undertow.
I cannot touch or feel her secret world.
She waves and laughs, gives herself to blue.
I wave back like an overboard landlubber.
She points at something in the blinding distance.
Is it me in a lost incarnation?
What heart am I, to fear her daring depths?
A dead fish floats by, one eye searching for God.
I owe her at least a stroke or two, and more.
So what if we're lost in the funhouse,
with nothing but mirrors to guide us?
I might be better drowned but I swim on.

The stranger I knew

He followed me each day,
that stranger who looked like me,
waited in the hall outside each class,
laughing at all my answers.
Some nights as I silently wept
under the shadows of forgotten stars,
I spotted him racing up and down the street,
setting stoplights on fire.
He blew a gold and silver horn
outside my window each dawn.
All the townspeople pointed at my fear,
and still he tapped on my windowpane.
I denied him entrance, did nothing
while my teachers trapped angels in words,
until the day I saw him point at you
as you tugged a balloon string to keep you from floating.
Then I stepped into my stranger flesh
through a door wide open to wounds.
Roses throbbed their longing in the sun,
and sweet winds came to whirl me undone.
You let free your balloon,
and touched my hand to other worlds.
Each planet escaped from prisoned night,
while ponds amazed themselves to diamonds.
And while you traced my new body
from shadow to bird to flight,
I saw him one last time,
stringing stars with songs of light.

The meaning of suffering at Utopia Amusement Park

might be wound round this merry-go-round
like some muse of all knowing
sings to me of all of us alone
and together riding magic horses
for eternity, this closed system of perpetual
motion, no sure destination, waiting
for the neon music to end, this machine's
predicable, creaky riffs, and fibrillating drum, turning,
turning, turning, intimations of mortality in the horses'
mouths screaming at the cotton candy moon
whirl round me swirl round the world swings me
free yet pulls me back, involves me, open and bound,
one foot in the stirrup, hands clutching the pole that
wounds my horse from heart to hoof as all my poems
fly free like drunken angels headed for a fall…
And the sad old lonely men and women
with eyes like faded butterflies, sitting this one
out, worn-out, turned inside-out by time so I see
all their secrets gone as a haiku breath, round and round
they fly with atoms and rocks and stones and trees
and Orion's maddened eternal hunt and they watch
fate's hammer trying to bang the bell, the chrome ball
going up and down and up like a nervous Adam's apple
and still that blasted bell never rings, no trumpet cries, no
second-coming Christ points the exit and my eyes roll out
like snake-eye dice in God's rigged game of chance I feel
my grip begin to loosen at any moment I might—be hurled!
right over the radioactive rollercoaster that rattles its bones

and shakes like a demented synaptic cleft.
Dostoevsky, worn down by time and Jew-hate,
is asleep at the switch, and the machine goes round
and round, until, like a Deist's God pocket-watch,
it must run down so down and sad to entropy.
Wake up, Fyodor! Show me how these children
will each snatch a golden ring, and not be cast away
to hunger and wars, bagged and tagged, pasted
obituaries in Ivan's private collection of pain,
his pointless quarrel with the God he can't believe in,
the one who keeps the dead bodies pure and clean
and even the usual Dostoevsky's desperate defense—
When in doubt, faint, faint in the inspector's office or
down the stairwell or in the bleak, bee-less ice caves
of Siberia, not even Prince Myshkin on his donkey has
the answer, since like his author he has his karma on
backwards—not pain and suffering, followed by angels and
bliss, but the blissful, aura flash of light so briefly cupped in
love, followed by the fall off some crazy cliff into endless night
doom like a million bath house spiders crawling up your eyes,
divine dive-down punishment for daring to hope to dream to climb
towards the high holy atomic detonation, death, the master
of worlds, the end of time unwound music of all your
hopes scattered —- a dropped bag of marbles splayed
across a floor stained with forgotten worlds and moonlight.
Everywhere I look, I see a wound.
I see Blake riding a tiger, predicting Nobodaddy's fall.
So teach me love, you horses of instruction.
Horses know the faith of journeys, spin the wheel
of suffering counterclockwise, whirl me back to the womb,
when I was too thumb-sucking dumb to be unhappy,
or fling me to the safety of bumper cars,
where pain is sacred to the bashed and creamed.

And though going nowhere fast has its advantages,
my horses of love, keep leaping for heaven forever.
I used to think you had all the answers,
your eyes as dark as a secret forgiveness.
Now help me hold on, hold on as this wheel
spins free to other lost worlds, stacked like endless
amusement parks learning to cry, since
holding tight is the only answer I know.

Memory balm

I close my eyes and return
to my grandmother's antique store,
where glass unbends the sight to visions,
where the shelves whisper their secret worlds,
where my grandmother hums whatever a dream means,
and silence holds time in a sweet embrace.
I go back, far back,
to escape the anger of words that bleed,
heal the wounds time carved in my heart.
and touch the purity of stained glass windows,
that change heaven's white radiance to life.
Whispers find a home here, the stopped clocks
ring the walls, each hand pressed to one
eternal hour. By day the sun lights each
crystal one by one. By night the moon
tendrils the lattice work, to bind, to bind,
to bind the past with love.
I need but a hint to guide me back.
I calm here, I descend and ascend with the light.
I am safe and sane again, for now, for now…
invisible here, where lost things come to meaning.
I wait and watch as the light turns and turns,
forever in its search through memory.

Signs in Samsara Town, 2023

The poor section:

“Condemned.”
“Eviction”
“Enter At Own Risk.”

The middle-class section:

“For Sale”
“Out of Business”
“Vote Trump”

The wealthy section:

“No Trespassing”

Letter to the editor of *The Samsara Times*

Editor: Samsara Town is going to Hell on a handcart. God's truth is not believed and there are lazy homeless people sleeping on our streets. Something's gotta be done before it's too late. Read the Book of Revelation, you'll see. This country used to have values and things. Nowadays They are teaching our children to hate their country. They force them to read books about things like slavery which really weren't that bad and ignore all the good things like how we are the richest nation on earth. They are turning our children against us. We all know how mailable our children are. Children can be taught to do almost anything, but They are turning them into little monsters. Samsara Town is going to Hell on a handcart.

Bedford Hunley
Not giving you my damn new address (yet)
Samsara Town

Samsara Town graffiti

“There’s no Samsara”

“Did you see that?”

“Help”

“Wish you were here.”

“Will kill for work”

“The world is like a ride in an amusement park. And when you choose to go on it you think it’s real because of how powerful our minds are…And we can change it anytime we want…Take all the money we spend on weapons and defense each year, and instead spend it on feeding , clothing, and educating the poor of the world…Not one human being excluded, and we can explore space together, both inner and outer, forever, in peace.”——Bill Hicks

“Poetry is never surreal. Poetry can never be surreal. It is the world that is surreal, and the poets just try to keep up.” —The Samsara poet

Elements of discontinuity

The Samsara National Bank,
its windows
a hundred dark eyes
watch The Ranger Theater,
its painted lawman
peeling from the brick
its blank screen
no longer seeing visions,
no angel light over the seats.
I walk the streets of Samsara town.
No one sees me
now that I'm old.
I like it this way.
I hear things
I would otherwise miss:
"What the Hell am I gonna do?"
"I can't even afford money."
"He doesn't really love me, I know he doesn't."
And the busses pull out and away,
a lonely face stuck in each window,
exhausted ghosts trailing behind.
And the wind comes, bringing rain,
and the raincoats flutter and twist
like pinned butterflies.
Is this all a dream
of the homeless man,
a chess table the roof of his house?
Is he tortured by the scent

of hamburgers and hot coffee
wafting from the Kewpee?

Does no one see him
but me?
No hunger like poverty.
The pigeons know,
cringing in the church bell tower
hiding from the bitter storm.
All of this samsaring
forms an endless meditation
as I fade into the mirrored windows
again, I come and go
at will, listening to the stories
confessing in the wind.

Does Hog River flow to divinity?

I cannot deny this:
Hog River is *here*, that's for sure.
It winds its way through Samsara Town
like some visiting stranger's signature.
It has no mythic pretext or portent,
nor requires one, and though it once
caught on fire, it is no Phlegethon.
Yet this might be all to the good.
Since without myth or medieval faith,
we'll have no need for wars or boiling souls.
Although I once witnessed a dead body
floating in it, when I was young and uneasy,
a Black man who'd been knifed by five white men,
then tossed to an anonymous death.
I think life might be less horrifying
if we had fewer cruel metaphors,
no more tragic fake horses, no more cities
sacked and burned, or old men blinded
for merely asking questions, no more sons
punished with death for loving to fly.
And for God's sake, leave the virgins alone.
I know Hog River is real,
but can it ever be divine?
Somehow I must learn to see death
as holy, and suffering, and loss,
and all those murdered without a why.
I will watch for clues, and keep them in my pocket.
I will walk these banks until I hear them sing.

Done gone blind

She enters Westgate Bowling Lanes
and all the pins quiver.
Her ball shrieks down the wood
and the pins are a fist-busted mouth.
She heads for a whiskey sour,
two eggs, boiled, a frown of bacon,
and toast half-burnt, deeply-buttered.
The counter man gulps at her approach.
Her metal cane sparks across the floor.
Patrons part before her
or, clutching in bands, turn into
bowling pins anticipating doom.
Now her cane whacks from side to side,
a psychotic metronome,
just missing the ears of her mastiff,
whose teeth are final pins of death.
She spins the stool top
until it obeys to just her height,
drains the whiskey, then winks
at her imagination in the mirror.

The pin-setter

He was the pin-setter,
at odds with their whole world.
They shattered, he built—
unseen, unheard,
his hands as sure as silence,
but they knew he was down there somewhere
under their lanes.
They rolled their black bowling balls
viciously at him, as soon as he finished
setting the last pin,
punctuating their contempt,
hoping to terrify him
or crash his face in,
such was their drunken rage.
They missed. He was perfect.
Every pin placed in precise alignment,
an arrow aiming straight at their hearts.
Their laughs came out like barks:
"That one got him!"
"Nah! You'll never get HIM."
"I thought I saw his face!"
Their Twentieth Century Lanes,
their rolling cannonballs like clenched fists
swinging at a grin.
Someone sent him to Vietnam,
and when he returned,
a shiny machine with hands like knives
had taken his job away.
You can still find him,

directing traffic in the downtown square
at midnight. You won't know his face,
and he never speaks, but he is the one
keeping the town from collapsing,
and dreaming every fallen leaf
returning to its tree.

The Cameo Bar, 6 a.m.

"Lucro privato non costituisce propesperita."

Their shift begins at seven.
The bar mirror watches them warily.
They do not sing
or crack dirty jokes.
Theirs is serious drinking,
a mechanical process
strong enough to last a day.
Each believes in his heart
that the system intends
everyone to succeed,
and no amount of pain,
disappointment,
frozen wages,
or busted unions will change their faith.
The struggle is, they say,
for freedom's rights,
a day's pay for a day's work,
no more, and perhaps a dream
that their children will do better,
move to somewhere outside Samsara Town,
if such a somewhere exists.
They are not killing time,
though time is killing them,
day by day, shift by shift,
punched-out time card
by punched-out time card.
It's a dog's life, all right.

They shrug, and await the whistle.
Their factory lives
by artificial respiration.
There are only six factories left
in Samsara Town. There are thirteen bars,
and thirty-three churches,
just to give God an even chance.

Toys For Tots

A lady with a nice cloth coat
drops a Barbie doll
in the cardboard box,
dusts her hands,
and turns away with a grin.
A man in a golf hat
drops a plastic fire truck
on top of Barbie,
checks his watch by the bank clock,
and hurries away.
An old lady
jams a hula-hoop down the back,
like she is stoking a furnace,
making sure it is visible
to passersby.
Later, a Mack truck will drive up,
an efficient volunteer leap out,
and toss the box with the rest
to deliver it to the south end
of Samsara Town.
Always the south end,
where the Standard Oil flares work all night,
drowning out the stars
and Hog Creek bends
round rusting cars.
Christmas Day will dawn
in the south end, south end,
and the children
will unwrap each present
believing it is new.

Mr. Smith's visit

Mr. Smith has arrived
from the organization
in a long sleek limo
with a one-eyed driver
who knows twice as much as he sees.
He invites himself in
with his buttonhole pin.
The neighbors don't know who you are.
But he's known you for years,
and he can pour you out like water.
Fingers his watch chain, you know, you
know. A notebook appears, with answers
that echo like lies, shakes his head,
sighs and shrugs, tsk, tsk…
While witches titter in the trees.
Oh, Mr. Whoever-You-Are,
your days came and went with the postman.
Mr. Smith tips his hat, it's time for that.
Come on now, get dressed, now, now,
you know you must. You must.

From *The Samsara Times*—date uncertain:

Samsara police yesterday discovered the bodies of a young man and woman in the front seat of a car on Industrial Drive. Autopsies are pending, but police stated that the as yet unnamed couple appear to have died from fentanyl poisoning.

From *The Samsara Times*—date uncertain:

WESTINGHOUSE to close Samsara Plant. Mr. Todd Null, president of the Samsara branch of Westinghouse Electric Corp., announced yesterday that the factory will close its doors permanently at the beginning of next month. The Westinghouse Samsara branch was built in 1924, and along with Standard Oil, U.S. Steel, and Samsara Locomotive, played a crucial part during the 1940's and 1950's at a time when this part of the country was referred to as "The Industrial Belt." Mr. Null stated that the plant's machinery is scheduled to be shipped overseas to a currently unannounced location.

From *The Samsara Times*—date uncertain:

SAMSARA LOCOS WIN SEMI-FINAL!

The Samsara Locos defeated the Ahimsa Angels yesterday 3-1 to advance to the championship series with the Shawnee Arrowheads. Center-fielder Jim Crockett scored a two-run homer in the ninth inning to win the game for the Locos, earning them the chance to win the first league title in the team's history.

The seamstress of sorrows

She sews and sews the tattered garment,
but the grieving mothers rend and rend,
the cries of lost children in their hair.
She sews and mends and sighs to herself,
but the mending and mending never ends.
Her tears long for rivers and seas.
She sews night to passion,
and faith to doubt,
but no garment warms an inner wound.
Her needles glide like swift fish,
weave sun to shadow,
memory to despair.
She sings of things that cannot be torn.
She can sew the inside of a silence,
but can never clothe the nakedness of sorrow.
Sometimes she whispers to the wind,
trying to confess her secret—
why she weaves the dark dream of our sorrow.

Minstrel obligations

Fossils shells are dancing with that skeleton
again. It's gotten to be a damn tradition.
Under a tambourine moon,
they yelp and clatter like a zoo,
explaining myths to the zodiac of fate.
I want them amscray, gone,
I'm tired of all their portents in the wind.
They are a facile weight, empty of love,
a persistence of bone and alone.
Let us seek the new our bodies crave.
Yet skeletons never tire of minstrel nonsense,
clicking and clacking like broken xylophones,
trying to pull a laugh from misery.
Fossil and Bones, that deluded duo,
who believe they are meant for eternity.
So bring your hidden self to sunlight.
Now is right for any faithful song.
And never mind old arrogant Bones,
his boasts of former greatness,
and fossil tales of triumphs on the seas.

If only...

"If's eternally."—Melville

I

If only the philosopher
did not begin with the answers,
then work back to the questions,
or keep inventing reality
by asking his questions...
Or if language, that drunken cowboy,
would stop staggering into the saloon,
roaring drunk with six-guns blazing,
to shoot holes in Truth's best hand all night...
If only God could find the present tense.

II

If only the universe
were not a vast, intricate nervous system
forever on the verge of breakdown,
or our bodies not made of treason,
turning against us piece by piece by piece...

III

I think what I mean is,
if this world is an illusion,
then it's a damned good one,
since it wounds and aches and
sighs and cries and screams and
bleeds and hurricanes and starves
and dies, dies dies...

IV

If only the first word spoken
by each fast-food patron at the drive-through
were not “Gimme…” The modern mantra.
Gimme-I-Me-Mine. Cranking up
the alienation machine one more time,
and turning me as lonely as the vulture
who drops down on the highway like a puppet on strings,
trying to get one bite of that dead cat.

V

No, I’m not expecting miracles.
I’m satisfied for now with minor acts,
everyday revelations that blow your hat off,
like losing your virginity in a rowboat.
Or a morning glory unfolding into light…
Or reading a book to find a better world…
or remembering how my Grandmother closed her eyes
on the front porch swing,
and swung so gently to the cicada’s song.

Return visit

Samsara Falls are downing to a doom,
turning, churning, rolling, roaring,
its meaning what you will
can happen, can be
or cease to be, the bottom
a distant, impish wink
of darkness,
of complicity,
a short cut to the bottom of the world,
a kind of faith,
like stepping from a cloud into the thunder.
Motion in stasis,
a pondering,
a white shroud suspended in air,
an endless drowning.
You could test it with that stick there.
Pick it up, feel its skin,
cup it gently as all love,
then let it go to forgotten.
There's the rub, then.
At least you are here,
at least you are now,
not something gone and done.
You are like a one-legged acrobat
suspended over Niagara Falls.
or a wounded crane
spending itself in flight,
this secret you hide between your words.

A brief history of man

The wars come
and the young men die
and the women write poems
to clean up
after every war,
and collate them
into books made of wise
Eighteen-century French covers
with rococo engravings in gold.
And the men were wrong,
dead wrong.
And the women are right,
living and right.
But then the next war comes,
raining bombs and poems,
and the collections grow,
whole libraries
of words and bodies,
under the turning knives of light.
Blood and sonnets,
living truth
and broken teeth,
the stacks crammed
with flesh and visions
we never learned what to do with.

A Polite Anarchists' Manifesto

I suggest:
That as a true skeptic questions skepticism,
and a true theologian questions faith,
so a true anarchist questions chaos.
and I would prefer:
that rationalists study physics so they may divest themselves of reason,
and historians explain Hiroshima to school children, and when they fail,
they must agree to seek honest work,
and Nazis be forced to march in Hell while singing "OO-EE-OO-AH-AH!",
and all national anthems be replaced with the Blues,
and draft boards replaced with checker boards,
and mushroom clouds replaced with magic mushrooms,
and NASA scientists turn their eyes around
so they may explore the universe within,
and leave the poor old moon alone,
and Queen Victoria shake hands with Jack the Ripper,
her dark secret lover, and ministers and bishops
follow a snail to Golgatha,
and Christ's life be remembered and honored, not his death,
and poor Blacks hooked on cocaine in the Hood
and poor Whites hooked on opioids in trailer parks
be appointed as police chiefs all over the country,
and cheerleaders cheer only for the poor,
and all strangers unveiled from their strangeness,
and all narcissists register for a soap box derby
without a hill,

and the four directions be switched four times a day,
to jam the superhighways, confuse the arrogant,
and end the Confederate Renaissance,
and a vaccine be developed against ignorance,
to end the samsara-merry-go-round.
and that as soon as grammatically possible,
"and" be placed at the end of each sentence,
just to keep our options open.

What eternity knows

Eternity cannot fathom itself,
senses itself only in the web
of a dragonfly's wing,
or the atomic dust of night moths
seeking the streetlight they dream is the moon.
The way a cicada shell
clings to earth and sky,
an emptiness in form,
or the way the firefly
enlightens what it cannot see.
And lightning is the skeleton of gods,
and the moon hides her darkness from the sun,
and a fence in a snowfield
divides nothing from itself.
You are the depths of your secret eye.
Eternity is vast but fragile.
Lovers can flame it with a single kiss.
That light-radiant, all-yielding
heaven of the body's imagining,
no poem is ever alone.

The sonless Father

How lonely must this god be,
who thinks all thoughts as one,
never imprisoned, never free,
and speaks his words in stone?

How lonely must this god be,
his breath a voiceless song,
who emptied his only garden,
then abandoned his only son?

How lonely must this god be,
whose eyes are shattered mirrors,
who watches, watches, all the night,
and never dreams nor fears?

I'd rather be Adam, lost in sin,
yet know my end, and how begin,
fulfillment through hunger, joy from despair.
Better crucifixion—than bodiless air.

In March some autumn leaves return

In March some autumn leaves return,
a very few, from beneath the melted snow,
neglectful of that fall so long ago,
and seeking innocent green.
The cold winds wind them into questions
or hurl them into backhand waves.
Can this be Spring?
Can they really be young again?
They are brown, brittle, vein-hardened,
claw for a hold as they scuttle down stones.
The winds fade and now they cling to roots,
accepting with sighs the need to feed the earth.

Nirvana hawk

Despairing wind caused by angry chrome,
ah well, dead Skyhawk on I-75,
its flesh like a busted cardboard crate of eggs,
battered and broken by an eighteen-wheeler,
an explosion of blood gone to entropy,
feathers scattered in dreamings of the moon.
The stars whisper it back to silence,
to ancient light dead in endless space.
I hold my vigil in the darkening field,
its mate praying or sleeping on a wire—
Does she wait for him to rise again in flight,
to soar and curve and cry and dive and kill?
And if these hawks and I find nirvana
even here, on this pain-highway of death,
you will know we're here, invisible
in plain sight, like this bird of longing omen
gone from this old forgotten world,
as dark blue winds sing the trees to sleep.

The bear that saw the world seeing

"Reality is unrealizable
while it exists…Poet, how
old is suffering?" -Bob Kaufman

Once there was a bear
in Faurot Park
in a seven-by-seven foot cage,
pacing time to eternity.
Little boys teased it, mocked it,
pelted it with snow balls.
It watched them all alone,
and its vision came with bars attached.
Then one day, many years on,
It finally saw the truth: The world
is the prison, the cage only our eyes.
We are inside-looking out, thinking we are free.
And now the bear is patterned in the stars.

The dharma balloon

This balloon longs for no distant shore,
is what it is in its own delirium,
God's tautology in whatever colors you wish,
changing its hue each time your view it
That way no single image becomes your prison.
That way it's quiet and free as a prayer.
The balloon floats over the limestone quarry,
guided by winds of its own desire
with no thought of fate or destination
and will not confess what it knows.
Its oxygen breathes for no one,
holding its breath as it glides the abyss.
My father's fathers dug this quarry
in the old dark earth that forgives no one.
It is a lonely depth of longing.
The vultures that hide their eggs here
long for birth and death, the sun for night,
the moon for its own hidden face.
This painful earth may never fade away,
but the balloon is content with time,
pulling sun, moon, stars and us behind it,
headed for Samara Town, and all that darkness.

The dream of an old poet sleeping in Samsara Park

A Seeker weeps beside an angry river,
his little raft and oar useless.
He sits in the dust and ponders
all the sad bones of this world.
He knows he'll never reach the other shore.
He looks up and Buddha is here.
"You are dreaming," he says.
"Ask me a question and dream yourself awake."
"How can I find the other shore," the Seeker asks,
when the river is raging and my poor raft no help?."
"What is on this other shore?" asks Buddha.
"I have heard it is the land of no more weeping,
where darkness leaves our bones."
"The answer is simple," says Buddha.
"Merely untie your raft, and throw your oar away."
"But how can I then reach the other shore?" asks the Seeker.
"You are already on the other shore," Buddha replies.
"You have been here all along.
The heaven you seek is in your every breath."

Confessions of a failed Bodhisattva

I

How to name this world holy
in a time of destructions.
How find a heaven in a field of blood…
And the pale fire moon is not death
but death's imagination,
sending a ghost through every window.
And yet my heart beats
with the pulse of crickets in the night
as they preach the temperature of darkness.
And I hear my blood rush in the conch shell tides
drawn from blue to green,
while the pain of memory folds into love.
And yet naming it Maya, Samsara,
or the dream of the Red King
won't make wounds go away.
Blood, my own blood, seems unreal
whenever it reveals itself.
Am I really part of all this flowing?
Calling it dream or illusion
won't bring back my wife, father, mother, brother,
however unreal their absence.
Every wind knows the silence of alone,
every star a white wound pinned to the sky.
What are we but museums of pain?

II

"And it is impossible that a being possessed of right understanding should regard anything as an ego."—Buddha

Yet to say a self does not exist
requires a self to say it.
Hence Buddha's remarkable loquaciousness.
He never stops speaking about the value of silence.
And if the ego does not exist,
what is this "I" that longs to come home?
And if I, as Buddha claims, exist in all others,
then how can I live safe in Nirvana
while they remain on the wheel of suffering?
It all comes down to suffering.
This is not a proposition from Wittgenstein.
From Job's cry to Snowden's last two words,
it all comes down to why.

III

The Four Noble Truths
I can never get past the first one.
The Noble Truth of Suffering.
I keep tripping over it
like an inept painter over his milk-soft brush.
What is noble about suffering?
It turned Lear to a mess of rags and weeds.
It took my family, bone by bone by bone.
Memory cleaves and weaves me into time.
I know suffering, like poverty, is ignoble.
I have seen the poor of Samsara Town
ground down to powder, their furniture
piled in streets like some obscene excretion.

So if I am to be saved,
I must first learn the language
Samsara speaks, and its people.
The stones that make their buildings mark their graves.
If only things were not such perfect allegories.
I can't pass Town & Country Flower Shoppe
without reading death in every bloom that blesses
weddings and funerals with equal indifference.
My only hope is the Bodhisattva, a shaman
who has attained Nirvana in one gone breath,
but refuses heaven till all are enlightened.
Till then he returns to this wheel of suffering
and again, and again, until the last sinner
is saved. I am perhaps that sinner.
I am no Bodhisattva, never been saved,
only lost, have not attained nirvana.
Yet if satori is everywhere,
I will search everywhere, even here,
carry my candle in brightest sunlight
until I see God.

Tathagata Akshobya

passes through from here to here,
signs his name on the wind, mountains, stars and moon,
while the Joker deals out the cards of maya.
Look at this world, a burning house,
and here we are, insisting
on the importance of our fingerprints.
The plan rarely goes according to plan,
though each word unfolds a possibility,
like the shifting patterns in winter treetops
nodding yes and no in the wind.
This world prefers a wide embrace.
Release your doves to magic.
The world is cicada, each shell a song,
comments on itself—look here, listen there—
God, like love and poetry, happens in time,
teaches us the radiant colors of anywhere,
shows us this world is paper-mache',
painted in flesh, blood and bone.
This world suffers from root to tip of twig,
and every real pain is illusion,
though it may feel like all hell,
cries to us from the torment-demented storm clouds.
How empty this sky, and we are fallen angels
learning to sing in the dark.

Night sky Tathagata

Delve the night to speak the spirit true.
Become a rumor of endless desire,
as two doves, spiraling into clouds,
capture the moon. What are these stars
but holes in the mask of God?
Here in Samsara Town,
eternity lives just upstairs,
and in the Schoonover Park observatory,
constellations study the astronomer,
the maya sky a scattered deck of cards.
In August the apocalypse looks down,
casting meteors in search of lonely graves.
Whispers of spun silver and gold,
reticent angels weary of hymns and despair.
Earth is best enough to find a heaven in.
The stars tonight may have been blown here
by a single autumn dandelion
bending its crown to the winds,
or a single white radiance
bored with all that purity.
Whether I ever find Tathagata,
or Tathagata somehow finds me
in only a mirror of my longing, no more,
I yearn to see and learn in waking things.
the way stars and fireflies
fade to silence one by one by one.

Satori in Wal-Mart

I

There is nothing in the mind
surreal as a firefly.
A true soul, he's open all night.
The self at arrival,
cannot be the same that departed.
Every return comes with a lie.
I move to unbind every circle,
safe from its clench of fear.
The only true roads are open.
The beginning must never be the end.
A snake with its tail in its mouth
feeds on its own desires.
I let myself become
whatever is around it
whenever I walk outside
I am Samsara Town,
each broken tenement window
watches lonely through my eyes.
Who speaks a city
is the city.
No voice but follows its echo.
Let the mind become
a mirror longing
for an image.
As the roots mirror the tree
the town lights mirror
the Van Gogh stars.
Light breathed into the blood,

deeper than any grave,
higher than God's creaky heaven.

II

But oh Hell, in Samsara Town
there are five identical Wal-Marts.
Civilization worships the same.
Overwhelmed with sales and despair,
I can tell the aisles and aisles
only by their numbers.
And yet this one little girl
wraps her scarf around a pumpkin,
says "This is who I talk to."
Bless me, Buddha,
with a vision equal to hers.
Somewhere in this sad labyrinth,
a place to call a home.

Editorial Page

Letters to the Editor of *The Samsara Times*

Dear Editor:
Samsara Town is going to Hell with a handcart. Our town used to be a great place to live when people knew their place. Now we have illegal immigrants and abortions running all over the place. God intended us to be separate it says so in the Bible. White and black, white and whatever—separate (but equal). Jesus loves the unborn. Crime is everywhere and people are afraid to go outside their doors. We need more prisons. What this country needs is mass incarnation. Lock'em up, I say. Our country is being destroyed by a conspiracy of liberals and secular humanists who are grooming our children to be pedophiles. This conspiracy is run by THE DEEP STATE, which is a secret society. Don't tell me you haven't heard of it everybody's heard of it. It is run by Globalists and Jewish-Communists bankers and they want to take all our guns and leave us to the mercy of strangers. I don't even recognize this country anymore. Samsara Town is coming a part at the seems.

Bedford Hunley
225 Pleasant Avenue
Samsara Town

The Samsara Times obituary page

Bedford Hunley, 66, passed into the arms of his Lord yesterday at Samsara Memorial Hospital. He had battled chronic heart disease for years. Bedford was a servant of his community, as reflected in his many heart-felt letters that appeared on the editorial page of this newspaper. He was also an avid hunter, and our local expert on the Confederacy, despite his Yankee origins. A graduate of Samsara High School, Bedford followed his local high school sports teams all his life. He lived and died a devoted Trojan.

Fence in snowfield

Master of weathers, somehow enduring,
this fence, seeking eternity,
must happen in space and time,
a graceful scar down a white canvas,
framed in frozen pine,
this brushstroke of sullen, frowning wood
hewn and cut and shaped and nailed in place,
a hundred crosses trudging up a hill,
a motion of breath and blood,
a dialogue between two worlds
opposite yet the same.
Relentless calligraphy signing the landscape,
seeking an horizon that recedes like echoes,
a plank fence with no idea
where it is going, or what, if anything,
it is supposed to be dividing,
as if a voice could secede from itself,
or a god from his own imagining.
It confronts you with a choice and here you are.
Can you chart it from origin to destiny?
Resolve its dilemma with a painted phrase,
or trace it to pure resolution?
It seems to be a question of perception,
whether we, like it,
can behold two worlds at once,
each world an opposite and mirror.
This is samsara, and if you could
tear it from the earth like a fish's spine,
you might end the division for good,

or you might end yourself with it,
as well as this artifice, this fence,
this poem of all longing,
this imagined self you desire but doubt,
for a oneness as gentle and lonely
as wings of angels turned to falling snow.

"Flower nevertheless" (Allen Ginsberg)

When will I learn the language of a flower?
Especially the trauma of this sunflower,
its shadow a broken god in Autumn,
its crown of bitter thorns,
and palsy shake in the wind.
And yet it binds
time to eternity,
weariness to gold,
and at sundown its shadow advances
and speaks to me in blood and ashes.
Perhaps we are all flowers nevertheless.

The star hidden in the sunflower

The star hidden in the sunflower
awaits its final wisdom.
Wrapped in silence,
it learns the patience of light years,
dreaming of the stars they left in darkness.
The sunflower arches towards its father
while the star dreams of the lonely moon,
and in its secret heart of diamond
yearns to climb from light to light
until all stars seed eternity.
Shadows descend. The sunflower drops
its guard, and the star escapes
in a gold unfolding, like fireflies
freed from a child's palm,
to weave the ancient language of the night.

Nirvana sometimes hides in Autumn

Autumn night,
outside my window—
apples thumping the earth...
Cold dark lake,
the only sound—
ducks nibbling the weeds.
Harvest moon,
the fat pumpkin
lighting up the porch.
October sky,
the stars
with clear, hard edges.
Dandelion seeds
floating towards the night sky
forming new constellations.
October,
a maple leaf
dreaming of its freedom.
Nirvana in Autumn—
what is death but whatever
makes us count to two?

Monster of ashes

Oh the great and terrible monster has died,
the one that rattled the stars, breathed ghosts,
devoured doves and lighthouses.
It tumbled and fell at last,
and its crash woke all skeletons to joy.
It kissed the earth with its poison breath,
spilled its dread hunger that feasted in flames
on every breath you dared——dead at last.
Look—
Its eyes are rotting poppies now,
blinded lookouts, sunken priests of pain,
x'd-out cruelheart caved-in ashes,
its blood boiling and bubbling obscenities,
its tail the hate it dragged everywhere,
even its tears are filth.
How long it dreamed you dead,
clawing its rage through your dreams,
its jail-teeth longing for your flesh.
How it hated you for finding each dawn!
It was only your love it wanted,
all your love to devour for itself,
to hoard as its private treasure
while you went begging.
Go now, walk up to it, watch it closely,
the size of a dead child.
Touch it now,
this demon of children and ashes.
It was this and no more,
only this great fear at last,
and no more.

Shadows

The shadow of a blind girl
seeks its way down a wall,
dreaming of things that shine.
The shadows
of December trees—
moonlit crucifixions.
The sunflower's shadow
is a great king
blessing his empire of seeds.
The shadow
of the red horse
is free from all the wars.
The shadow
of the white horse
touches day to night.
The shadow
of the green horse
is all the Spring becomes.
The shadow
of a butterfly
traces an invisible hand.
The crow shadows caw samsara, samsara,
as they weave your home town with darkness.

Let

Let the poet's strong line enter the world.
and trace itself back to memory.
Let its brushstroke illuminate earth, wind, and sky,
and send a neon moon to the lonely.
Let breathe the litany wind in trees,
and hear the song of the whirling leaves.
Let every poem conceive a life,
and like a loving parent let it go.

Thou art That

And so I go on searching,
the lunatic moon my lantern.
God must be somewhere,
a silent child hiding all alone,
or perhaps an aged songstress
singing my blood from roots to stars.
The stars are exiles
wandering in circles,
the North Star seeking an invisible hand
to guide us home,
and the bare trees pray for alighting angels.
Someone said this universe is a dream,
but he was lost so long ago
no Bodhisattva can remember.
So I lie in the patience the grass keeps,
watching for clues cast by fireflies.
Perhaps if my eyes turn deep within
they will find the starlit path to heaven
waiting breathlessly for footsteps.

Nirsamsarvana

The jeweled universe
reflected in the wings
of a dragonfly.
The heart's quick tracing
of the sudden flight
of the redbird.
A transcendent
shorthand,
a Buddha balanced
on every twig of a Winter tree,
a word, a world
spun in the palm of the hand.
Moonlit epiphany in a cat's green eyes.
or wink of a wound that knows you to the bone.
These images bind us to earth and pain,
the blood dreaming of a rose.
When memory is a wound,
why should heaven be white?
When memory is blessed and blessing,
when we were children,
and walked within the inner world of things,
heaven was blue and green and all embracing.
I trace two worlds longing to be one.

Sattva prayer

My son's cockatiel
tips one eye at me,
black and willed as a seed,
and asks "Whataru?"
A girl with a blue umbrella
enchants a vision of herself
in a store window glazed with rain.
Her umbrella's spokes,
thin and strong as bat wings,
bend deep with every wind.
These images
float in pure space,
and time a penny clutched
in the emptiness.
While my own bones creak and crack when I rise,
remind me of origins and ends
and the poem is born in blood and marrow.
Old women search for sound fruit
in the grocery bins,
their hands soft as peaches,
sure as alighting birds.
With these everyday visions I may endure
what is and what may come.
The heaven I know abides in winds,
where forever so brief of time I am free.

Gerard Manley Hopkins:

"Under the world's splendor and wonder
lies the hidden world
sacred keeping its secrets
hidden from the blind"
see only what they want to see,
longing only for the known
knows only itself,
feeds full on its own image,
visionless as Pluto.
Yet earth-wise desires
await the patient seeker
knows how to dig for stars
inscaping for light
to redream constellations
in new patterns.
To let each world look back,
unselving you to other
outrider planets,
rove-over meteors
spun from darkness
or teachings of the leaves,
all things spell-bent,
imperfect and pure.
All things unseen, unsung,
longing for a voice to find them.

Sutra in green

The praying mantis's
diamond mind
waiting, a patience,
mother of darkness,
sister to the fates,
knowing her prey will alight.
The moonlight upholds her,
her silence
in perfect balance with the stars.

The cicada as earth and sky

The cicada, born in middle-earth,
tunnels through centuries to light,
turns sun from blue to green to gold.
Escapes itself to become itself,
learns by heart the ancient songs of trees,
chanting secrets to the night.
One morning it is gone,
its song melted into moonlight.
Its empty shell clinging to a mystery.
While we remain, alone in time,
humming beneath Winter winds,
pondering clues of broken things.

Bird lights

Inside each bird is a light.
The light is singing.
It sings of distances
between breath and silence.
At night it perches,
wondering back at what it sang by day.
And only then are its distances achieved,
its fear folded in the sleep of wings,
and its loneliness cast to a million galaxies.

Shasei

Autumn wind,
a flame,
a sudden leaf
engoldening the air
Winter wind,
treetops groaning with the strain,
the whole woods
crying for the Spring.
Spring wind,
leaf buds like ripe berries,
and the sparrows perch here
waiting.
Summer wind,
leaves turn green to white,
the top branches
where most never look.
Every leaf contains a word,
a tree a language,
the roots a hidden world
aching with desire.

The radiant gist

Scatter the sun
to find the constellations.
The tensile starlight
reaches for your heart
long after the stars themselves
have faded into darkness.
This night sky within
eludes all systems,
a hidden moon behind the one we see,
its zodiac as wide as thought.
Call it a new constellation:
A man with a blue guitar.
Yet this meteor, the poem,
can only happen in time.
Yes, that's it, this flame
the eternal, wrapped inside
the falling, the poet, earth-bound,
reading signatures in wind-blown leaves.
The radiant gist—
meteors are thoughts
randoming their way in search
of a meaning, a satisfaction,
a world to call their own.

Winter song

Be kind,
cold wind—
We are both strangers.
Cat in freezing rain—
First its breath,
then its cry.
December snowmen
melting
into tombstones.
This snow——
a sudden
memory.
Star
pond
star.
The moon
gently
testing the water.
Trust them
the stars
come on their own.

Samsara Town haiku

Every laundry drier
is samsara, nirvana
the empty, turning center.

Under
the Salvation Army sign
an old man shakes his head.

Abandoned
railway station,
now a homeless station.

Post office
green with envy
of silence.

Prostitutes
waiting in the cold
outside The Imperial Inn

Dome’s Peanut Shoppe,
its scent
golden.

This pitcher's mound,
all that remains
of Summer dreams

Crumbling brownstones—
well aware
they were once well off.

Faurot Opera House—
Without lights,
without music.

Library patrons
surfing
the internet

My family home—
strangers
live there now.

Trick or Treat—
A little girl asks me:
"Why are you old?"

Samsara Town night

Don't worry
bullfrogs,
I'm lonely too.

She ascends,
the ladybug,
heading for Mars.

A snail
crawling
up my telescope

Cabbage moth,
wings folded
under the moon.

Clouds come and go—
a world
dreaming itself.

Leftover leaves

The winter pulls back in fear and wonder
unveiling green, and busy wings,
but the leftover leaves are lost and homeless,
and scuttle about like crabs.
How many winters have I left?
I can count behind but not ahead.
Leftover leaves scrape their empty questions.
What hand unblessed can save them from the void?
Now I let them creep close, closer,
daring to be near.
Let the wind invoke them into flight,
seeking an origin in empty air.
At night the wind, the bone-aching wind,
returns. Candlelight bends like a praying nun.
The leftover leaves whirl hopelessly through the dark,
and I must learn the wind has many wings.

A late word of encouragement

You walk more surely than you know.
Your shadow is not a punishment.
You will do.
Come then and take my arm.
A book is where two people meet,
and where we both must live.
And please don't go looking for suffering.
Suffering will find us on its own.
Pain is endlessly patient.
"Pain is a dream," wrote Saint Kerouac.
All right, true enough, but if so,
I hope to soon awaken.
I walk to mystery now,
waiting for darkness to call.
Perhaps revelation is silence.
And samsara?
I have come to suspect it
weaves us round nirvana in love.

Last chapter

I have walked this town many times,
telling the sad: “Don’t worry, it’s only dream.”
But these days I wonder
if it’s not more like a poem
we’re all trying to cobble together.
I am an old man now
who knows
he’s turned into a book
he began long ago,
a few pages
missing
that might have solved the mystery,
the ending yet unwritten
pages penned years in the past
that once seemed strong and clear
and no longer make much sense.
Words are dreams.
Silence the final poet.
All I know—
I must seek each day to listen.

Their art

Wasps are spinning their nest
in what used to be my back window.
The wind blows,
my mind trembles.
They enter and exit their perfect caves,
pulsing some code as yet unclear.
They mold their wings down tight,
bullets that pierce and return.
I cannot read them yet,
my blood races too much.
Their eyes are black seeds
glinting in the morning sun.
I stand, approach, press palm to glass,
though they ignore me,
too busy stitching their lower heaven.
My breathing slows, and finished,
they swirl round and round their creation,
though some, the guards,
line the sill like perfect punctuation.
The glass is cool pressed to my face,
the sun a throbbing vacancy of blue.

www.ingramcontent.com/pod-product-compliance
Lightning Source LLC
LaVergne TN
LVHW091119150826
845673LV00002B/892

* 9 7 8 8 1 1 9 2 2 8 4 2 3 *